APPRECIATION

An Essay

By

WILLIAM LYON PHELPS

First published in 1932

British Library Cataloguing-in-Publication Data
A catalogue record for this book is available
from the British Library

CONTENTS

WILLIAM LYON PHELPS

William Lyon Phelps was born on 2nd January 1865, in New Haven, Conneticut, United States.

Phelps earned a B.A. in 1887, writing his thesis on the Idealism of George Berkeley. He then gained an M.A. in 1891 from Yale and his PhD from Harvard in the same year.

During his time a Yale, he offered a course in modern novels which brought the university considerable attention both nationally and internationally. This was quite controversial at the time and Phelps was pressured to give up the course, but eventually, due to popular demand, reinstated it outside the official curriculum.

In 1892, Phelps married Annabel Hubbard, sister of childhood friend Frank Hubbard, and the couple moved to the family estate overlooking Lake Huron. Phelps christened it "The House of the Seven Gables", after the Nathanial Hawthorne story of the same name.

He became a very popular figure at Yale but also as an inspirational orator. He went on lecture tours that drew large audiences, speaking on the virtues of modern literature. He also preached regularly at the Huron City Methodist Episcopal Church and attracted such large crowds that the church was remodelled twice in five years to accommodate them.

Phelps published many essays on modern and European literature, including titles such as *Essays on Modern Novelists* (1910), *Some Makers of American Literature* (1923), and *As I Like it* (1923).

After his retirement from Yale in 1933, after 41 years of service, Phelps continued his public speaking, preaching, and writing a newspaper column. He also sat on book selection committees and acted as a judge for the Pulitzer Prize for literature.

His wife, Annabel, died from a stroke in 1939 and Phelps died four years later, in 1943.

APPRECIATION

AS I DESCEND deeper into the vale of years, it becomes increasingly clear to me that I am a happier man not only than the average, but happier than many of those who are younger, healthier, stronger, and richer than I. And I say this after making due allowance for the fact that most people seem to hoard their happiness, as if they were afraid of spending it. They seem unwilling to look cheerful or to admit that they are happy.

Although the circumstances of my life have been fortunate, I believe the chief source of my happiness lies in my gift of appreciation. It is one more illustration of the law of causation. As I have ten times more appreciation than the average man or woman, it does not surprise me that I have more happiness.

On the ninth day of August 1712, Mr. Addison contributed a poem 'to the London Spectator which may be found today in nearly all the hymnbooks. It begins

"When all thy mercies, O my God, My rising soul surveys, Transported with the view, I'm lost in wonder, love, and praise."

Imagine a modern novelist or playwright or literary critic saying that! Imagine the average man or woman thinking it! For, in the most tremendous age of miracles the world has ever known, the average man has lost his capacity for wonder. In a time when the world is drawn more closely together by common need than ever before, the majority of our writers have forgotten the meaning of the word love; while many regard the habit of praise as the mark of a shallow and plebeian mind.

Another stanza in Addison's poem is especially significant:

"Ten thousand thousand precious gifts

My daily thanks employ,
Nor is the least a cheerful heart,"

That tastes those gifts with Joy. Addison thanked God for many precious gifts that came to him, but particularly because he had a cheerful heart. He could not have appreciated the panorama of life without that, any more than a blind man could appreciate the paintings of Rafael or a deaf man the songs of Schubert.

The prevention of disease consists in finding and removing the cause; the way to happiness consists in finding the key which will unlock the door of the prison in which so many of us dwell.

While a certain amount of money is essential merely to live, and the sum must be increased in order to

widen the range of one's enjoyment, it is unquestionably true that there are persons who apparently have everything and are not happy, while there are others with modest incomes and cheerful hearts.

As I can enjoy looking into a shop window without the slightest desire to possess anything it displays, so I believe one can enjoy many things without owning them or wishing to own them. If God offered to make me a present of the sunset, so that it would be my sunset, flare only on my property or flare more effectively on my property, I should decline to accept the gift. I appreciate the beauty of the sunset more than if I owned it.

I am not making the trite suggestion that instead of longing for what they have not got, people should make the best of what they have. There is hoary wisdom in such a suggestion, but it irritates more persons than it helps.

Appreciation as I understand it is something quite different and more rare. For by appreciation I mean to enjoy not only everything you possess but also everything else.

Appreciation is not self-satisfaction, complacency, or conceit. Those three qualities are centripetal, drawing all things toward the core of selfishness; while appreciation is centrifugal, throwing out ardours that make invisible contacts with beauty; forgetting oneself as completely as one does in listening to ravishing music.

The less satisfied one is with oneself (as distinguished from one's possessions) the more satisfied one will be with everything else; and the reverse is true.

The curse of modern life, the poison that turns honey to gall, the cause of the dull, stupid, despondent mood in which so many people live and move and have their being, is a lack of appreciation. Many go through life with their eyes, ears, and minds closed.

"Blessings brighten as they take their flight," said the Reverend Doctor Edward Young; but why should they? Why not consciously enjoy blessings while we have them, instead of spending our days and nights in vain regrets?

Life, with all its tragedy, frustration, disappointment, and unsatisfied desire is not so bad as many philosophers say it is. Very common experiences prove it. One may go to bed in a despondent frame of mind; but in the hour before dawn one has a horrible dream. One wakes up in a sweat of fear; then one hears the good old trolley-car go by, or the milkman leaving his bottles, and one rejoices; it is the cheerful, normal round. The dream was an hallucination. One is free. Real life seems good by contrast.

But real life seems good by contrast not only with horrors, but with a state of perfection. Ludwig Fulda wrote a play called Schlaraffenland where a wretched boy, clothed in rags, chronically cold and hungry in a miserable hovel, fell asleep and dreamed he was in a land of warm sunshine. Birds were flying very close to him and moving so slowly through the air that he reached out his hand and took one. It was a broiled chicken. He ate it with gusto, and another and another. Whenever he was hungry, the air was filled with perfectly cooked chickens. He looked at his rags-suddenly a broad door swung open, and there was a wardrobe filled with handsome and well-fitting clothes; all he had to do was to choose. Whatever desire he had was immediately gratified. For some time he was happy; then he began to be vaguely bored, dull, uninterested; this feeling of weariness gave way to increasing unhappiness. Finally, with a yell of agony he woke up-and found it was all a dream. He was cold, he was in rags, he was hungry; and as he looked around his miserable room, he exulted. "Thank God, I am back on the good old earth!"

Many men and women who find life melancholy and unsatisfying, suddenly catch the influenza. As the sufferer lies in bed with fever, unable to get up, he does not long for riches or fame or beauty or perfection. He wants only to be what he was last week. If he can have back his normal health and activity, it is all he asks. That state which a few days ago seemed nothing to be grateful for, now appears exceedingly good.

The point I make is, why wait for a bad dream, or an iridescent dream, or a fit of sickness to appreciate daily healthy existence? Why not enjoy these things while we have them? I mean consciously enjoy them. Well, I do.

G. K. Chesterton is profoundly religious; the late Arnold Bennett was not. But both men found rich enjoyment in daily living. They lived with gusto, with a keen relish. Arnold Bennett's attitude toward life was a chronic wonder, amazement, delight; even the innumerable little gadgets of modern existence pleased him enormously. While as for Mr. Chesterton, he says he hopes he will never be too old to stare at everything. Appreciation begets gratitude and gratitude begets happiness. You cannot store or save gratitude; economy there is fatal; if one tries to save gratitude, one may find it gone; but the more one gives, the more one has left. In the same number of the Spectator that contained his poem, Mr. Addison wrote, in the formal style of his day,

There is not a more pleasing exercise of the mind than gratitude. It is accompanied with such an inward

satisfaction, that the duty is sufficiently rewarded by the performance. It is not like the practice of many other virtues, difficult and painful, but attended with so much pleasure, that . . . a generous mind would indulge in it, for the natural gratification that accompanies it.

Even as a little child, I responded gratefully-and usually with surprise -to any acts of kindness or to any courtesies from older people. Even now I find no difficulty in feeling appreciation for generosity, hospitality, or praise; my grateful response is as spontaneous as the deed or word which it acknowledges. On a certain occasion many years ago another college professor and I were entertained at a magnificent house over the weekend. When we came to go, it was as natural as breathing for me to express to our hostess how much I appreciated her kindness; and I meant it. I told her I should never forget it, and I never have forgotten it. My colleague, being of a quite different temperament, looked at the lady and spoke one word-" Good-bye."

When we had left the place, he said "What a horrible effort it is to be polite! and it doesn't bother you at all." Now this man is a staunch and loyal friend-only he does not get half the fun out of life that I do, because he has no gift of appreciation.

I must have been born with an unlimited gift of appreciation; and it has grown by what it feeds on. It may be that I am too easily pleased -that I have not a sufficient amount of discrimination. I admire summer and winter, sunrises and sunsets, I like moonlight and even better star light, I enjoy classic and Gothic and Colonial architecture, I like great tragedies, great comedies, great farces, I revere the courage of a Ney and the courage of a washerwoman. If I were more fastidious, if only a very few objects and only a very few persons received my approval, then perhaps I should have a higher reputation as a discerning critic. And if I almost never praised anything, then on the rare occasions when I did, even though somewhat grudgingly, release admiration, my praise would be worth more than it is now. But think of all the happiness I should lose! Many ignorant men believe criticism means fault-finding. They think the best critic of a poem or a play or a composition of music, is the man who searches sedulously for defects and limitations, rather than the man who discerns what is good and praises it. I am willing to admit that some books and plays please me that evoke no admiration in others.

And many books and plays, which are highly praised by others, disgust me beyond words; which is why I can find no words to express my opinion of them. I believe the best praise one can give any work of the imagination is to say it is worth criticising; and by criticism I mean neither faultfinding nor denunciation. The art of criticism is the art of interpretation; interpretation requires insight.

Furthermore, while I get more happiness out of the gift of appreciation than I should from being overfastidious, I must admit there are certain persons who seem to find sincere pleasure in depreciating and ridiculing every book they read, every play they see, every musical performance they hear. Various attempts at creative art are valuable to these critics as a target is valuable to a marksman, or a head at Donnybrook Fair. It is an opportunity for the exercise of destructive wit; I suppose there is a certain pleasure in wielding a bludgeon -the joy of the slapstick. Some critics obtain pleasure not only in this exercise, "Gregory, remember thy swashing blow," but in the reputation in this fashion acquired; yes, even in the fear they inspire. For while most people are neither formidable nor dangerous, most people secretly like to be so regarded. It may be a damaging admission; but no man, woman, or child has ever been afraid of me.

Yet, granting the definite pleasure in conscienceless murder, I do not believe that the critic whose main weapons are irony, sarcasm, and ridicule, gets half the fun out of life that I have. And I also believe that this attitude of depreciation, except where it is accompanied with constructive suggestions, is usually sterile. These are the critics whom Thomas Hardy called "sworn discouragers of effort."

Indiscriminate praise-even indiscriminate sympathy-would, in matters of art, be worthless. But the fact that I prefer to spend my time and energy in the appreciation of good things rather than in the denunciation of unworthiness, does not mean that I am without a standard. It does not take me long to discover that in a package of ten new novels, nine ought not to have been published; that (judging by the advertisements) of motion pictures, the majority are vulgar; that when I turn on the radio to hear something I am eager to hear, I wheel my way to it through a morass so sickening that it seems as if it must produce softening of the brain.

Indeed, I think some of our modern writers have no standards at all. Their pictures of slime are of little value because there is no suggestion that there ought to be, as of course there is, a higher level of character and environment. Dickens gave us pictures of low life, but we always knew by reading his pages that it was "low" because it could be measured by an experience of what was better. Mr. Santayana commends Dickens because he always knew the difference between right and wrong. His good people are really good, his evil people are really bad. I do not believe a novelist, playwright, or critic can judge human nature if he does not know any difference between right and wrong.

The greatest of all German critics, Goethe, said the chief qualification for a critic was Enthusiasm. I believe this to be true. A critic of music must begin by loving music; a drama critic must begin by loving the theatre; a literary critic must begin by loving books. Love is the foundation of understanding; and enthusiasm the wellspring of intelligent appreciation. Is it not possible that some critics who began by loving their chosen field of art have gradually lost that love; and with the loss of enthusiasm has vanished also quickness of insight, sensitiveness to impressions?

And if this is true in matters of art -music, theatre, books- it is surely true of life itself. One reason so many people are not so happy as they ought to be is not because of their lack of material things-but because they do not respond to beauty in nature, and charm in men and women, as they used to. The power of appreciation should grow with one's advance through life; life itself does not grow less mysterious, less beautiful, less interesting; it is not the object, but sight and hearing that are dull. If you find you are not so much interested "in things" as you used to be, the trouble is with you, and must be corrected. Fortunately it can be.

Encouragement is creative; irony is destructive. Encouragement does not mean falsehood, and I am not suggesting that one should say a manuscript, a book, a picture, a singing voice is good when one inwardly knows it to be otherwise.

But as a professional teacher, I have had abundant opportunity to observe the developing power of encouragement and the sterilizing effect of scorn. People endeavour to live up to praise and to justify it; whereas cynicism or indifference will often extinguish a faint spark of talent. I remember, more than thirty years ago, asking a student to remain a moment after class; I told him his written work was excellent, far superior to the average. His face was flooded with surprise and joy. He said in all his years in school and college that was the first time any teacher had given him a word of encouragement. Well, his subsequent career more than proved his worth. But the point I make is, that while my passing comment gave him happiness, his happiness in receiving it was not so great as mine in giving it. And the main object of this little book is to show that one road to happiness lies through appreciation.

Most men and women do not sufficiently realise the sensitiveness of our fellow-creatures. J. M. Barrie says that sometimes, after having read a venomous attack on his work, he has written a bitter rejoinder (which he knows how to do), gone out into the street to post it, and with his hand over the letter-box, suddenly reflected that perhaps his victim will receive this epistle after he has sat up all night with a sick child, or after he has just received a shattering financial disaster or after the physician has told him he has a fatal disease.

Now, while most men and women are not in an acute crisis of tragedy, everyone has something to worry about. I do not care to add to his torment. The reason I do not exercise the power of adverse criticism is not because of lack of ability. Mr. Addison said the reason he did not tell vile stories was not because he did not know any. My ability to hurt another man's feelings is quite sufficient. Once I was urged by the editor of a college paper to criticise the contributed articles severely-" Please be unmerciful; it will do them good!"

Accordingly I selected one short story for especial condemnation. The undergraduate author himself gave no hint that he was hurt. It was one of his friends who told me that it was the first time this man had ever had anything in print; he had feared it was not good; and my censure had hurt him so that he would never try again. It appeared that he had a natural tendency to discouragement and low spirits; a few years later he committed suicide. It is not pleasant for me to reflect that during his short life I had added to his suffering.

It is surprising to those who have not fully considered the weaknesses of human nature how very sensitive are the majority of human beings. Many people, both great and small, prominent and obscure, seem unable to endure adverse comment, irony, ridicule, insult, without intense and prolonged suffering. To say of any person that he was harmless would seem such faint praise as almost to make him ridiculous; he might feel justified in resenting it. But really, if such an adjective could accurately be applied to any man or woman-it never can-it would be a marvellous tribute.

We hurt somebody almost every day; intent upon our own purposes, we jostle and shove our way through the complexities of social intercourse, leaving wounds more acute than if we jammed an elbow into somebody's eye.

No decent man would kick a cripple; but there are many who suffer more from ridicule and adverse criticism, yes, even from lack of consideration, than they would from a bodily injury. There are many unfortunate men and women who have no particularly sensitive spot, because every spot is sensitive.

Even men of genius have confessed that they suffer more from one adverse criticism than they gain in happiness by ten favorable reviews. I was amazed when I learned that writers of established fame-Tennyson, Hardy, Henry James-suffered excruciatingly from attacks by reviewers whose opinion was of no importance. If gold rust, what shall iron do?

If men and women of talent and popularity are so sensitive to an ill wind, what must be the anguish of those who are not sure of themselves, who are struggling hard, and with constant misgiving, to do better work? I know as a matter of fact that there are many distinguished artists who never read a word written about them, because they cannot endure an unfavourable remark.

Hence when a young actor or singer or playwright or composer takes up a newspaper and sees himself held up as an object of derision, he suffers torture inexpressible. A woman whose first play was savagely reviewed wrote me that when one fails in business or in athletic attempts, people are sympathetic; but when one writes a play that fails, the critics put the playwright in a position as if he had done something shameful in the presence of the public.

Anyone who writes a book or a play certainly invites attack; it is as if he stood stripped and bound in the marketplace, where every passer had a right to throw something at him. "Oh, that mine adversary had written a book!"

Once more, I do not mean that a critic, in order to spare the feelings of anyone, should dishonestly praise what is not worth praising. But in transfixing a victim with the critical pen, it is not necessary to put poison on the tip. And wherever it is possible to give encouragement or to see a high purpose even through failure, it is well to remember the good results that come from sympathetic insight and appreciation.

This need not be applied only to professional criticism. It applies to the give and take of daily life. Every boy and girl, every man and woman is an object of observation and therefore of criticism. Appreciation stimulates and depreciation discourages.

Most men and women need courage.

In these matters as in the general question of happiness, I am more fortunate than the majority of people; because in the first place I am more pleased by praise than I am downcast by blame; and in the second place, abuse and slander and misrepresentation do not give me deep or lasting pain. When it has been my unpleasant occupation to read or hear harsh attacks on something I have said or written or done-attacks meant to be devastating, to destroy my peace of mind-these blows annoy me no more than mosquito bites. If I refrain from scratching, the poison will not sink in, the bite will soon be forgotten. As soon as an injury is forgotten, it is as if it never had been. Adverse attacks and ridicule are not agreeable, but one can train oneself to endure them; even to feel no prolonged resentment.

Here again is the enormous blessing that comes from hard work. I am really too busy to spend much time contemplating my bruises. There is always the next thing that must be done.

The late Commodore William J. Matheson, one of the most interesting men I ever knew, read to me an abusive letter he had just received. I made the conventional remark "Don't let it worry you!" He looked at me in astonishment: "Why, such things never worry me. You can see by the letter that it is the other fellow who is doing all the worrying!" We exaggerate the power of our enemies and the importance of their attacks. Many persons who have been "criticised" imagine that everybody on the street is thinking of their predicament; but no, these people are all thinking of something else.

One should make the most of all sources of happiness no matter how trivial they may seem; they are not trivial if they produce joy. When I was a schoolboy, I enjoyed the Saturday holiday so much-every Saturday-that along about three o'clock on every Friday afternoon I felt a rising tide of bliss-the bliss of anticipation. And as I have never been easily disappointed, Saturday was usually just as good as I thought it would be. Outdoor games and all that sort of thing-winter and summer-were an inexpressible delight.

As for tremendous events, like Christmas and the Fourth of July, they were a delirium.

Yet as I look back on childhood and youth, happy though I was, I have no regret that they are irrevocable; I have no sentimental yearning for the past. I walked and ran and skipped and leaped through those flowery roads and advanced into a country quite different but more interesting; because there was not only more to appreciate, but my power of appreciation had developed.

The difference between my happiness as a child and my happiness as a man, is that then I always wanted something unusual to happen, some excitement to take me out of the routine. Saturday was the golden day of the week. Now my hope is that nothing different will happen. I hope only I may be able to keep in sufficient health or vigour to go on with the daily routine. Instead of waiting for the holiday, every day is interesting. I enjoy the hot bath in the tub as I used to enjoy the old swimming hole.

Perhaps those men and women who are still looking for excitement, something with a "kick" in it, are mature only in body. They have not developed.

Perhaps in their search for excitement, they are neglecting sources of happiness more easily attainable. For as many persons are either afraid or unwilling to admit that they are happy, so many men and women are ashamed or afraid to admit their appreciation of simple and ordinary things. True mental development consists largely in the discovery of what has been there all the time. It may be as I have said-that I am not sufficiently discriminating; yet experience proves to me that my enjoyment of elementary means of entertainment does not detract from my enjoyment of the best; even though I enjoy the best more than the second best.

I am transported by the symphonies of Beethoven and by the operas of Wagner. Yet that does not lessen my enjoyment of Gilbert and Sullivan, of a drum and fife corps, of a brass band. As I grow older, I find Shakespeare constantly more thrilling; the beauty and felicity of his language are enchanting; yet I have tremendous relish out of a good detective story. I shall never forget my excitement in seeing Edwin Booth in The Merchant of Venice, yet I love the circus and everything in it.

I admire Lindbergh and all spectacular heroes; and I admire humble men and women, who, in adverse circumstances, show courage and cheerfulness in obscurity. Browning said, "O world as God has made it! all is beauty: And knowing this is love, and love is duty."

Nature is always beautiful; and as one becomes older, nature becomes more and more beautiful. I am writing these words in New York. From my room on the sixteenth story I saw the sun rise over the East River this morning, and my heart exulted.